HIGH STYLE ON THE HIGH SEAS

HIGH STYLE ON THE HIGH SEAS

PASSENGER SHIP INTERIORS

WILLIAM H. MILLER

FONTHILL

To dear friends Jim Brochu and Steve Schalchlin, both of whom are masters of creativity and talent—each a great artist is his own right

Fonthill Media Language Policy
Fonthill Media publishes in the international English language market. One language edition is published worldwide. As there are minor differences in spelling and presentation, especially with regard to American English and British English, a policy is necessary to define which form of English to use. The Fonthill Policy is to use the form of English native to the author. William H. Miller was born and educated in the United States; therefore American English has been adopted in this publication.

Fonthill Media Limited
Fonthill Media LLC

www.fonthillmedia.com
office@fonthillmedia.com

First published in the United Kingdom and the United States of America 2020

British Library Cataloguing in Publication Data:
A catalogue record for this book is available from the British Library

Typeset in Minion Pro 10pt on 13pt
Printed and bound in England

CONTENTS

FOREWORD

I WELL RECALL SITTING in a large, soft chair, and, although with a good book in hand, I watched fellow passengers. There was a sense of "commerce" about them—coming in from outer deck, returning from a game of shuffleboard, heading off to the writing room or a morning round of bridge, or that stroll around the promenade deck. We were mid-Atlantic, on a calm, sun-filled day in August 1958. With my family, we were aboard the palatial *Queen Mary*—and happily traveling in grand first class. There were polished veneers, leather chairs and oversized sofas, and a lighted map in the dining room that depicted the ship's position. We had crossed to Europe months before on another grand Atlantic liner, the *Nieuw Amsterdam*. She too was palatial and stunning: Moroccan leather ceilings in the dining room, Murano chandeliers and live music from a balcony during dinners. Indeed, these ships and their first-class quarters were like hotels, but hotels that moved. They were superb, even magical, and they provided the most wonderful transport—from one place to another. I thank my good friend Bill Miller for creating this book that reminds us of ocean-going grandeur and fantasy!

James Cameron
Chicago, Illinois
Summer 2018

ACKNOWLEDGMENTS

L IKE DESIGNING AND DECORATING passenger ships, it all takes many hands—a "crew" if you like. Creating this book has included many friends and acquaintances, who are deserving of an appreciative mention. My sincere appreciation to all!

First of all, thanks to Alan Sutton, Jay Slater, and the expert team at Fonthill Media for taking on this project. And very special thanks to James Cameron for this generous Foreword and to Anthony La Forgia and the late Norman Knebel for their exceptional contribution with photos and illustrative materials.

Further thanks to the late Frank Braynard, Luis Miguel Correia, the late Richard Faber, David Hutchings, Arnold Kludas, Anton Logvinenko, Rich Turnwald, and the late Everett Viez.

Companies and organizations that have assisted include Carnival Cruise Lines, Companhia Colonial, Cunard Line, French Line, Hamburg America Line, Hapag-Lloyd Collection, Holland America Line, MSC Cruises, Moran Towing & Transportation Co., Nedlloyd, North German Lloyd, P&O, Photofest, Port Authority of New York & New Jersey, Royal Caribbean Cruise Lines, Steamship Historical Society of America, and the World Ship Society, Port of New York Branch.

INTRODUCTION

ACK IN THE 1960s, I became a regular visitor to the New York City piers—to Luxury Liner Row. Young and enthusiastic, friends (from the newly organized World Ship Society branch) and I were often waved aboard the great—and sometimes not so great—liners. We did not have to pay the 50-cent boarding fee. Dockside officials and guards knew us. We were not passengers or even friends of passengers, just enthusiastic ship buffs.

We would cross those canvas-covered gangways, connecting pier and ship, and often enter into an enchanted world—the luxuries of an ocean liner. We would tour the ship from end to end, but we usually concentrated on the public rooms and outer, open decks. Standing beneath the funnel of, for example, the *United States* or *Queen Mary* was thrilling. Eventually, those throaty whistles would sound, thirty minutes before actual sailing. Those well-known words now applied: "All ashore that is going ashore!"

Each of the liners, except in the cases of some sisterships, were different. Each had its own ambience, its own personality. The styles spanned through the decades. There were the dark, heavily wooded interiors of the *Stavangerfjord*, *Berlin*, and *Vulcania*. There was the British Deco of the *Queen of Bermuda*, *Queen Mary*, and *Queen Elizabeth*, and perhaps a more European Deco on the *Nieuw Amsterdam*. The sleek look of '40s moderne onboard the *America* and the modified, post-war Deco of the *Caronia*. The likes of the *United States*, *Independence*, *Santa Rosa*, and *Brasil* offered the simplistic Yankee contemporary of the 1950s. Then there was the stylized Mediterranean look of the '50s onboard the *Cristoforo Colombo* and thematic touches such as the "Zebra Room" aboard the Greek *Olympia*. The likes of the *Bergensfjord* and *Gripsholm* presented the "clean" look of Scandinavian styling, while the *Rotterdam* blended luxury with cozy comfort and then there was the great success of the refitted, pre-war/post-war *Hanseatic*. In the '60s, the *France* had a simplistic, almost sterile style in place, while the likes of the *Michelangelo* and *Oceanic* blended ultra suede chairs, tubular lighting, and contemporary Mediterranean art. With Formica, cup-style chairs, and colors such as lime green, the *QE2* was dubbed "floating Carnaby Street" by several journalists. By the '70s and '80s, ships such as the *Cunard Princess* and *Nordic Prince* hinted of mass-market cruising—very metallic, low ceilings, and small cabins. However, by 2004, the *Queen Mary 2*'s interiors revived the grandeur of the past, with sweeping stairwells, high ceilings, and gleaming chandeliers. By 2017, the diversity of the current cruise generation was expressed in the mega-sized *Norwegian Gem* and *Royal Princess* and gold-plated luxury in ships such as the *Silver Whisper* and *Crystal Serenity*.

These days, and far from the New York City waterfront as well, the cruise business is booming. More people are taking to the high seas than ever before. By late 2017, some 100 new cruise ships were either under construction or on the drawing board. The year also witnessed the introduction of the largest liner ever; the *Symphony of the Seas*, of Miami-based Royal Caribbean International, was ceremoniously floated out at her builder's yard, STX, at St Nazaire in France. Costing some $1.5 billion, the ship broke all records and weighed in at 230,000 gross tons. She measured 1,188 feet in length and 215 feet in width. Used in Miami–Caribbean service, on seven-night cruises, she had the largest capacity yet—6,870 "guests" in all.

On eighteen decks, there are 2,775 staterooms, twenty-four passenger elevators, and no less than seven on-board "neighborhoods"—named and themed as Central Park, Boardwalk, Royal Promenade, Pool and Sports Zone, Vitality at Sea,

Entertainment Place, and Youth Zone. Highlights are the Ultimate Abyss, a ten-story slide; the Perfect Storm with a trio of water slides; and Splashaway Bay, a children's water park. There are six dining areas and ten specialty restaurants.

The likes of the *Symphony of the Seas* is extraordinary. She is special, innovative, sets a standard, and is a great and grand successor to these earlier passenger ships.

Passenger ships of today are almost all stunning—lavishly designed and decorated in often eye-opening decor. There are large, Las Vegas-style showrooms, multi-tiered dining rooms, indoor promenades, and soaring atriums and lobbies. Cabins range from indoor rooms, but with reality walls displaying the seas outside, to twin-level suites and penthouses with the likes of private dining rooms and personal gyms—and the list of special amenities could create a long list.

In this book, I have a made random and diverse selection of passenger ships—from noted Atlantic liners to colonial steamers to third-class migrant quarters. Hopefully, it will, in photos, show something of an evolution—a century or so of ocean liner decor. So, sit back and scan the pages—and you might "hear" the whistle sounding. A voyage is about to begin—*High Style on the High Seas*!

Bill Miller
Secaucus, New Jersey
Winter 2020

1900–10:
POTTED PALMS IN THE SMOKING ROOM

GERMAN FOUR-STACKERS (1897–1906)

They were the first of the superliners, the first of the so-called "floating palaces." By the last decade of the nineteenth century, the Germans—with growing technological and industrial might—were determined to surpass the dominant British, especially on the high seas. The North German Lloyd as well as the Hamburg America Line, rivals in their own right, were committed. Lloyd's effort came first when, in the fall of 1897, their 14,349-grt, 655-foot-long *Kaiser Wilhelm der Grosse* was commissioned. Immediately, she captured the attention of the entire world, was dubbed "the wonder ship," and ranked as the largest as well as the fastest ship afloat. She crossed from the so-called Channel ports to New York in just short of six days. The Germans established a design pattern aboard the 22-knot ship, the first of the so-called "super liners," by grouping the funnels in two pairs. It made these German ships more recognizable and had design elements as well—there was no need for four funnel shafts piercing through lower-deck public rooms. The *Kaiser Wilhelm der Grosse* was followed by the successively larger *Deutschland* (1900), *Kronprinz Wilhelm* (1901), *Kaiser Wilhelm II* (1903), and finally the *Kronprinzessin Cecilie* (1906).

Splendor on the seas: the rich, ornate style of Germany's *Kaiser Wilhelm II* of 1903. (*Author's collection*)

LUSITANIA AND MAURETANIA (1907)

Both are immortal ships—the *Lusitania* because of her tragic demise; the *Mauretania* as one of the most beloved ships of all time. Using different shipbuilders, the *Lusitania* came from Scotland's River Clyde, from the John Brown & Company shipyard. She was launched in July 1906 and quickly dubbed the "Lucy." The *Mauretania*, dubbed the "Maury," came from the Tyne, from Newcastle. Reflective of these big Cunarders, her accommodations were arranged for 560 in first class, 475 second class, and 1,300 third class. Their first-class quarters were especially splendid—furnished with fine woods, marble fireplaces, and luxurious carpets.

Tragically, the *Lusitania* was torpedoed and sunk on 7 May 1915. The *Mauretania* sailed on, to great popularity, until 1934. Afterward, she went to the breakers at Rosyth. Some of her wood panels and fittings later found their way into a pub and a film studio in the UK.

The biggest and fastest liner afloat, Cunard's *Lusitania*, berthed at New York's Pier 54. (*Anton Logvinenko collection*)

On the following page:

Above: A breeze-filled afternoon: the Palm Court Veranda aboard the *Mauretania*. (*Author's collection*)

Below: Relaxing on a mild Atlantic day: the very top deck of the illustrious *Mauretania*. (*Author's collection*)

2

1910–20:
THE FLOATING PALACES

OLYMPIC AND TITANIC (1911–12)

The *Titanic* is perhaps the most famous liner of all time—unquestionably because of her tragic end. The "unsinkable ship" sinks: the sinking of the supposedly unsinkable *Titanic* on 14–15 April 1912 has made the ship immortal. The ship and disaster have been the subjects of hundreds of books, magazine articles, TV documentaries, a Broadway musical, and, in 1997, James Cameron's billion-dollar blockbuster film. A total 1,522 perished in the *Titanic* sinking, and the 705 survivors represented a scant 32 percent of all those onboard.

The 45,324-grt *Olympic* was the first of White Star Line's three "mammoth sisters" and the first company liner with four funnels and ranked as the biggest ship afloat when commissioned in 1911. But, unlike the *Titanic* and their larger-still fleet mate *Britannic* (1914–15), the 882-foot-long *Olympic* had a long and largely successful career. A victim of the Depression of the 1930s, the *Olympic* was sold in 1935 to British scrappers.

The first-class smoking room of White Star Line's *Olympic* (1911). (*Norman Knebel collection*)

FRANCE (1912)

She introduced, in ways, the high and often innovative decorative styles that came to be associated with the Compagnie Générale Transatlantique, the French Line. Her superb decor prompted a nickname: "Château of the Atlantic." At 23,666 gross tons and 713 feet in length, the *France* was the first French super liner and France's first and only four-stacker—one of the Edwardian era's "floating palaces." Intended to be named *Picardie* and then *La Picardie*, she was launched as the *France* in September 1910 and completed in April 1912. Her maiden voyage took place just days after the *Titanic* tragedy. Rather interestingly, at the time of her delivery, there were four French ships also named *France*, while a fifth was British.

French style: the imposing first-class dining room—with grand stairway—aboard the *France* of 1912. (*Author's collection*)

IMPERATOR/BERENGARIA (1913)

She was Teutonic splendor, might, the pre-World War I German bid for trans-Atlantic supremacy. She led the way to bigger and bigger liners.

When completed in May 1913, Hamburg America Line's *Imperator* was a ship of immense, almost extraordinary, proportions for her time—52,117 gross tons, 919 feet in length, and able to carry up to 4,594 passengers in four classes. Taking three years to build, she was actually the first of three successively large behemoths. The 54,000-grt, 950-foot-long *Vaterland* followed a year later, in 1914, and the 56,000-grt, 956-foot-long *Bismarck* was scheduled for 1915 (but was never completed for German service owing to World War I). Hamburg America Line wanted every distinction other than record speed with its three giant ships. At first, they succeeded—the general public marveled at the mighty *Imperator*.

The *Imperator* did have some serious blemishes, however. She was soon found to be top heavy and easily rolled, even in the calmest seas. Consequently, her towering funnels were cut down by 9 feet, interior decorations were refitted with lighter materials, and tons of cement was poured along her bottom. But, in the end, she was never quite free of her fragility.

She could carry more passengers than any other liner afloat—her 4,594 passengers were divided as 908 in first class, 972 second class, 942 third class, and 1,772 in steerage.

The *Imperator* was very lavish in first class: lounges, salons, grand dining room, and—in a creation of marble, tile, and bronze—the Pompeiian Bath. It was the most lavish indoor pool and even included a second-deck spectators' gallery and, as an annex, a gymnasium.

Château at sea: the smoking room aboard the *Imperator/Berengaria*. (*Norman Knebel collection*)

The fresh sea air: enjoying the open decks on the *Berengaria* in the 1920s. (*Everett Viez collection*)

$10 per person to America: steerage on the *Imperator*. (*Hamburg-America Line*)

Immigrant children arriving in New York, among the 12,000 arrivals per day in 1912. (*Hamburg-America Line*)

But one of the great ironies of the Atlantic passenger trade was that while the highest attention, luxury, service, and food were provided for first and even second-class passengers, the real profits came from the third class and steerage passengers they carried to America. Steerage required less, and, therefore, it meant less cost to the ship owners. Even though most immigrants paid an average $10 per person for the crossing in the years prior to the First World War, vast corporate profits came from these fares.

The giant *Imperator* survived the First World War, but then was ceded to the Allies, to the British, as reparations in 1919. In her second life, as Britain's *Berengaria*, she was one of the most popular liners on the Atlantic. For example, she was often thought of as "floating Hollywood"—more film stars, it was said, preferred her. One American tycoon so liked the *Berengaria* that he booked his favorite suite on board for ten years. Another lady reported that her dog was more indulged and spoilt on this Cunarder than any other liner. The *Berengaria* endured until demolished in 1938.

AQUITANIA (1914)

She was dubbed "the ship beautiful." She was very good looking on the outside, but especially so on the inside. Her interiors were high luxury. There were the likes of the Caroline smoking room and a two-deck-high dining room.

After World War I, the *Aquitania*—which had a passenger capacity of 2,200 by the mid-'20s, divided as 610 first class, 950 second class, and 640 tourist class—was immensely successful. Evidently, her reputation went beyond her splendid decor but was also based on service and was said by some Atlantic travelers to be the very best afloat. Generally, all Cunarders enjoyed enviable accolades for their services to guests. "The *Aquitania* had the advantage," wrote the late John Malcolm Brinnin, "of a crew trained in a sort of father-to-son heritage of stewardship that marked whole families in Liverpool and Southampton. They gave service on a scale of British tact, grace and professionalism that positively dazzled American travelers."

She was originally built as a larger, refined version of the earlier, 32,000-ton *Lusitania* and *Mauretania*. Also a four-stacker and one of that generation of "floating palaces," the *Aquitania* weighed-in at 46,000 tons. Overall, she was Cunard's direct competition to White Star Line's *Olympic* and her sisters and the three German giants: the *Imperator*, *Vaterland*, and *Bismarck*. The 901-foot-long, 3,230-passenger *Aquitania* had a long and distinguished career—thirty-six years of sailing, service in two world wars, and, when scrapped in 1950, she was the last four-funnel liner, the last of the "floating palaces."

The grand setting of the *Aquitania's* dining room. (*Norman Knebel collection*)

3

1920–30:
THE LONGEST GANGWAY TO EUROPE

MAJESTIC (1922)

The biggest yet of mastermind Albert Ballin's "Big Three," she never actually sailed for the Germans—for the mighty Hamburg America Line. Instead, she sat out World War I in quiet solitude at her builders' yard at Hamburg before being ceded to Britain as reparations. Her maiden voyage, in 1922, was actually for the British—for the White Star Line as the *Majestic*, the world's largest liner until the *Normandie* appeared in 1935. As the White Star flagship (like the *Imperator*/*Berengaria* at Cunard, the pride of British companies, but in fact German built), the *Majestic* was hugely popular. She was the second fastest liner on the Atlantic and often carried record numbers of passengers. She was fondly dubbed the "Magic Stick."

Gathering of the great liners: New York's Chelsea Piers in the late 1920s. *From left to right*: *Île de France*, *De Grasse*, *Pennland*, *Olympic*, *Baltic*, and *Duchess of Atholl*. (*Author's collection*)

The world's largest ship—the *Majestic* takes a turn in the big graving dock at Boston. (*Anton Logvinenko collection*)

The foyer and entrance to the main lounge aboard the *Majestic*. (*Norman Knebel collection*)

HOMERIC (1922)

Intended to be the *Columbus* of the North German Lloyd, she sat out the First World War as an incomplete hull. After the Armistice in November 1918, she was placed on the Allied reparations list and was passed to the British, to the White Star Line, and became the *Homeric*. Used in the company's express service between Southampton, Cherbourg, and New York in the three-ship team that included the far larger *Majestic* and *Olympic*, the *Homeric* later became a well-known cruise ship. Her career was far too short, however. After entering White Star service in 1922, she was a victim of the Depression and was sold to shipbreakers in 1936. The 34,351-grt ship had seen only thirteen years of service.

Above: A skylight ceiling: the first-class lounge aboard White Star's *Homeric*. (*Norman Knebel collection*)

Right: During the winter, off season, and then especially in the Depression years, the big liners were often used for cruises. (*Norman Knebel collection*)

The
MEDITERRANEAN
CRUISE 1931

THOS. COOK & SON
WAGONS-LITS CO.

BY SPECIALLY CHARTERED

S.S. HOMERIC

LEVIATHAN (1923)

While the new flagship of the entire American merchant marine, the *Leviathan*'s roots were in Germany. Built at Hamburg as Hamburg America Line's *Vaterland*, she was commissioned in the spring of 1914 but saw little service before being left at her pier in New York harbor when the Germans went to war in August 1914. Later seized by the Americans, she returned to service as the war's biggest troopship, USS *Leviathan*. Later restored as a liner, she had a comparatively unsuccessful commercial career under the "Stars & Stripes." After little more than ten years of service, she was laid-up in 1934 and then scrapped four years later.

Luxurious isolation: the sitting room of a suite aboard the *Leviathan*. (*Author's collection*)

Above: Deck games on Cunard in the 1920s. (*Author's collection*)

Right: Economical and affordable, low-fare travel in tourist and third class became very popular in the 1920s. (*Norman Knebel collection*)

S.S. REPUBLIC

*Y*OU will be delighted with the pleasant staterooms on this comfortable "one class" cabin ship. Note the attention given to details which provide every convenience. This room is typical of the splendid low cost accommodations offered by the United States Lines.

COLUMBUS (1924)

She was Germany ship of "revival" in the early '20s. After the destruction and then seizure of German ships in 1918–19, the country lost all but one of its noted big liners. The former *Deutschland* of 1900 had been revived, but only as the migrant ship *Hansa* in 1920. The Germans, notably North German Lloyd, were allowed to keep the *Columbus* and complete her for a revived "big ship" luxury service to New York (from Bremerhaven via Southampton and Cherbourg). The 775-foot-long *Columbus* had actually been intended to sail as the *Hindenburg*, sister ship to the liner first named *Columbus*, but ceded to the British and becoming the *Homeric* in 1922. Consequently, the intended *Hindenburg* was completed as the "second" *Columbus*.

Two decks high: the main lounge aboard the German *Columbus*. (North German Lloyd)

RELIANCE AND RESOLUTE (1920)

Rather grand-looking ships, both had been built by the Germans, sold to the Dutch and then the Americans, and finally returned to German ownership. Three-stackers with solid appearances, they sailed the North Atlantic, between Hamburg, Southampton, Cherbourg, and New York, and they were noted—especially in their later years—as very popular cruise ships, especially for long, luxurious cruises.

The Winter Garden with satin-smooth dance floor onboard the *Reliance*. (*Norman Knebel collection*)

DUILIO AND GIULIO CESARE (1923)

In the early '20s, Italy moved into the "big leagues" of trans-Atlantic liner trading. These 24,200-ton sisters were something of a beginning. Commissioned in 1923, they were the nation's largest liners yet. They were a response to the need for bigger, faster, and more luxurious ships on the important run between Naples, Genoa, and New York.

MONTCLARE (1922)

Built by Canadian Pacific Steamships in the early '20s, the *Montclare* and her two sisters were practical, conservative, unpretentious Atlantic passenger ships. They were intended largely for the westbound migrant trade from Liverpool, Southampton, and Glasgow. Later, during the Depression in the 1930s, they were used in inexpensive, pound-a-day cruises from Britain—carrying travelers to the Canaries, Madeira, Spain, Portugal, and, in summer, to Scandinavia.

Left: The long gallery on the Italian *Duilio.* (*Norman Knebel collection*)

Below: A four-berth third-class cabin on Canadian Pacific's *Montclare.* (*Author's collection*)

ALCANTARA AND ASTURIAS (1926–27)

They were Britain's biggest and finest liners on the South Atlantic run—from Southampton southward to Rio de Janeiro, Santos, Montevideo, and Buenos Aires. Royal Mail's business looked promising in the mid-'20s. Voyages by then had to be grander, more comfortable, and faster. The business of transporting the business class—merchants and traders, bankers, and technicians—was all important.

Beginning in the winter of 1926, Royal Mail added the sleek, squat-funnel pair of *Asturias* and *Alcantara*. Company directors and designers decided to experiment with a new form of propulsion then coming into vogue. They surpassed Sweden's 17,000-ton *Gripsholm,* commissioned in 1925, as the largest and most powerful motor liners afloat when they were completed.

But their Danish-constructed Burmeister & Wain diesels proved in inadequate, and so both ships had to be re-engined eight years later, in 1934, using classic steam turbines. Their service speeds were increased from 16 to 18 knots.

First class (for 410 passengers aboard the 22,071-grt *Asturias*) was especially palatial, catering to grand and demanding travelers, aristocrats, and rich businessmen. Her public rooms were lavish, being done in splendid British and empire styles, and included a two-deck-high dining room that could seat all first-class guests at one time. There was also a Moorish-style smoking room, a paneled library, and a 29-foot-long, tiled indoor pool.

Right: Exotic flavor: the Moorish Lounge on the South America-routed *Asturias.* (*Norman Knebel collection*)

Below: Sailing for Rio: the main lounge on the *Alcantara* of Royal Mail Lines. (*Norman Knebel collection*)

CONTE GRANDE (1927)

The 25,600-ton, 1,718-passenger *Conte Grande* and her near-sister ship *Conte Biancamano* were two prime Italian liners of the mid-'20s. Both were built for Lloyd Sabaudo, a company later integrated in the early 1930s as the retitled Italian Line. In first class, they were especially lavish. The first-class main lounge, with a dance floor, was done in a varied interpretation of Indian Mogul, Arabian nights, and ancient Babylonia. Few liners offered such intricate, highly detailed decoration. In America, similar decoration was being used in some of the new motion picture palaces.

The highly ornate and rich styling of the *Conte Grande*'s music room. (*Norman Knebel collection*)

Eastern styling: the indoor pool aboard the *Conte Grande*. (*Norman Knebel collection*)

CAP ARCONA (1927)

Germany, namely the Hamburg-South America Line, had strong interests in liner services to the East Coast of South America—Rio de Janeiro, Santos, Montevideo, and Buenos Aires. While there was significant first- and second-class clientele, these German liners stopped in Portugal and Spain *en route* and so profited from a large third-class trade. Building successively larger passenger ships, the 27,000-grt *Cap Arcona*, completed in 1927, was the culmination. Big and fast, she was the most luxurious German liner sailing between Europe and the South Atlantic. Altogether, she carried 1,315 passengers—575 in first class, 275 in second, and 465 third.

German style: inter-connecting first-class public rooms aboard the Hamburg-South America Line's *Cap Arcona*. (*Author's collection*)

ÎLE DE FRANCE (1927)

The great divide: few ships had more personality—rather, a more distinctive personality. She was also the ship that created the great decorative divide. Her interiors were done in 1920s moderne, a style first seen in the 1925 International Exhibition of Modern Decorative & Industrial Arts in Paris. The *Île de France* began an era of new, trend-setting decoration, a style later dubbed Art Deco. In his book *The Only Way to Cross*, author John Maxtone-Graham called the *Île de France* "the great divide from which point ocean liner decoration reached forward rather than back." Art Deco at sea became the rage and was soon also called "ocean liner style."

When the 43,153-grt *Île de France* was completed in the spring of 1927, she ranked as the sixth largest liner afloat. She was the flagship of the French merchant marine, said to be the best-fed liner on the Atlantic, and carried more first-class passengers than any other liner. She was one of the most important ships of the twentieth century—and one of the most popular and beloved. The 791-foot-long ship resumed service after heroic trooping duties during World War II, was restored in French Line service in 1949, and then was scrapped after thirty-one years of service in far-off Japan in 1959.

Right: Welcome aboard! The main staircase and grand staircase aboard the innovative *Île de France*. (*Author's collection*)

Modern Greek temple: the Art Deco styling of the main restaurant on board the *Île de France* in 1927. (*Author's collection*)

MALOLO/MATSONIA/ATLANTIC/QUEEN FREDERICA (1927)

Built for California–Hawaii service, few ships have had longer and more successful careers. She endured for almost fifty years. She went on to become the *Matsonia*, *Atlantic*, and, finally, the *Queen Frederica*.

Off to Hawaii: the main lounge on Matson Line's *Matsonia* (1927). (*Norman Knebel collection*)

STELLA POLARIS (1927)

Likened to the royal yachts of Europe, the *Stella Polaris* was a pioneer of select, luxury cruising. She was the predecessor to the likes of today's six-star cruise lines such as Seabourn and Silversea. Smaller, but select!

The 5,000-grt *Stella Polaris* was designed to resemble a European royal yacht. She carried only 165 passengers, who were looked after by 165 crew, and did almost nothing but long, luxurious, globe-trotting cruises. Owned first by the Norwegians and (from 1952) by the Swedish Clipper Line, the sleek *Stella Polaris* sailed for over forty years before being sold and becoming a moored country club in Japan. Sadly, she was later to return to Scandinavian waters, but sank while under tow in September 2006.

The sitting room of a suite aboard the yacht-like *Stella Polaris* seen in the 1950s. (*Norman Knebel collection*)

SATURNIA AND VULCANIA (1927-28)

They were extremely ornate in decorative style, they were proud motor liners, and they both gave long and distinguished service.

Built for the Trieste-based Cosulich Line and later transferred to the Italian Line, they were primarily used in service from the Adriatic. After World War II, they resumed service, sailing between Trieste, Venice, Dubrovnik, Patras, Messina, Naples, Barcelona, Gibraltar, Lisbon, the Azores, Halifax, and New York. On board the *Vulcania*, accommodations were grouped as 279 first class, 257 second class, 310 third class, and 1,350 fourth class. Fares in 1939 from Italian ports to New York were posted from $110 in first class and $60 in third class.

Colorful artwork depicting the near-sisters *Saturnia* and *Vulcania*. (*Norman Knebel collection*)

An artist's rendering of the upper decks aboard the 1927-built *Saturnia*. (*Norman Knebel collection*)

Grand, ornate styling: the so-called vestibule aboard the *Saturnia*. (*Norman Knebel collection*)

Palace at sea: the ballroom aboard the *Vulcania* of 1928. (*Norman Knebel collection*)

The bedroom of a grand first class suite aboard the *Vulcania* of 1928. (*Norman Knebel collection*)

Deck games on board the *Vulcania*—and enjoying the mild mid-Atlantic weather. (*Norman Knebel collection*)

Roman style: the lavish indoor pool on the *Saturnia*. (*Norman Knebel collection*)

AUGUSTUS AND ROMA (1927–28)

Swimming on deck! Built in 1927–28, these 32,000-ton sister ships were the biggest Italian liners yet and the largest yet built in Italy. Of note, the *Augustus* ranked for a time as the world's largest motor ship.

Cruising on Italian Line's *Augustus*. (*Author's collection*)

Right: The ballroom aboard the *Augustus*.
(*Author's collection*)

Below: Shipboard comfort: a first-class stateroom on the
Augustus. (*Author's collection*)

KUNGSHOLM/ITALIA (1928)

The biggest Swedish liner yet, she was a popular, class-divided Atlantic liner, as well as an all-first-class cruise ship. During World War II, she became the US troopship *John Ericsson*. Beginning in 1948, she became the *Italia* for the then newly formed Home Lines.

Above: The lobby on Sweden's *Kungsholm* of 1928. (*Norman Knebel collection*)

Left: Swedish American Line became well known for their long, luxurious cruises. (*Author's collection*)

DUCHESS-CLASS (1928–29)

A quartet, these ships were designed purposely for Canadian Pacific's seasonal Liverpool–Montreal service and alternate off-season cruising. Smart looking and well decorated, these 20,100 tonners—named *Duchess of Atholl, Duchess of Bedford, Duchess of Richmond*, and *Duchess of York*—were built by the famed John Brown shipyard on the Clyde. They were preludes to the larger *Empress of Japan*, created for Canadian Pacific's trans-Pacific service in 1930, and for the larger, grander *Empress of Britain*, commissioned in 1931 for combined Atlantic service and world cruising.

The entrance hall and elevators on the Canadian Pacific *Duchess* liners. (*Norman Knebel collection*)

BREMEN (1929)

The *Bremen* and her near-sister *Europa* were long, low, sleek, powerful, and the embodiment of the description "ocean greyhound." In many ways, they were spectacular ships and, of course, symbolic of the rebirth of German shipping little more than a decade following the devastation of World War I. Germany lost, either through combat or to Allied acquisition, almost all of its passenger ships. The *Bremen*—immediately succeeding as the fastest liner on the Atlantic—was a great symbol of rebirth.

Left: By 1929–30, Germany's *Bremen* and *Europa* were the fastest liners afloat. (*Author's collection*)

Below: Grand hotel—the main lounge on the *Bremen*. (*Hapag-Lloyd collection*)

40

A quiet afternoon: the library aboard the *Bremen*. (*Hapag-Lloyd collection*)

EUROPA (1929–30)

While the *Bremen* went on to have a shorter, less fortunate life, the *Europa* endured—she had two separate careers, one German and the other French. Seized by the invading Americans as Nazi Germany collapsed in May 1945, this much-neglected super liner was later ceded to the French as reparations and was rebuilt and restyled as the *Liberté* for the French Line.

Left: Artistic labels were applied to suitcase and especially those great steamer trunks. (*Author's collection*)

Below: Nights at sea: a masquerade party on the German *Hamburg* in 1929. (*Hapag-Lloyd collection*)

~4~
1930–40:
COLE PORTER MUSIC AND THE SMELL OF EXPENSIVE FRENCH PERFUME

LAFAYETTE (1930)

She was not large or powerful or especially luxurious, but one of the more moderate Atlantic passenger ships dubbed the "cabin liners." Cabin-class liners, without a first-class designation, could offer lower, more appealing fares, especially in the Depression-era 1930s.

Right: Vast, fold-out deck plans: the French *Lafayette* of 1930. (*Norman Knebel collection*)

Below: The music room aboard the 1930-built *Lafayette*. (*Norman Knebel collection*)

5. *Intérieur du Paquebot "LAFAYETTE"*
Le Grand Salon de Musique
Vue d'ensemble

BRITANNIC (1930)

As history had it, she was the last survivor of the great White Star liners. Completed in 1930, she was passed over to Cunard-White Star in 1934, survived World War II, and later resumed sailing between Liverpool and New York. When she was sold to shipbreakers in Scotland in late 1960, she was the last liner built for the original White Star Line.

The first-class dining saloon aboard the *Britannic*. (*Author's collection*)

DEMPO (1931)

Dutch colonial links out east, to the East Indies in particular, supported a fleet of passenger ships until the 1950s. The two biggest and busiest firms on that run were the Amsterdam-based Nederland Line and Rotterdam Lloyd, expectedly headquartered in Rotterdam. Just as the worldwide Depression set in the wake of the Wall Street Crash in October 1929, both companies were building their largest, finest, and most luxurious liners yet. Nederland Line was creating the *Johan van Oldenbarnevelt* and *Marnix van St Aldegone*, while Rotterdam Lloyd was building the sister ships *Baloeran* and *Dempo*.

Off to the faraway Dutch East Indies: a first-class bedroom on board Holland's *Dempo*. (*Author's collection*)

JOHAN VAN OLDENBARNEVELT (1930)

Colonial service: "She was so dark on the inside—it was as if she was decorated in chocolate and cocoa. She even smelled dark—of coffee and tobacco. She was different, truly Dutch and quite exotic in ways," recalled ship historian Everett Viez. Completed in 1930, she was the largest liner yet on the colonial run between Amsterdam and the Dutch East Indies.

The dark, chocolate-like colors of Amsterdam—the main lounge on the *Johan van Oldenbarnevelt*. (*Nedlloyd*)

EMPRESS OF BRITAIN (1931)

Few big liners have conveyed the overall image of size, might, and total luxury better than the *Empress of Britain*. "She was a true ocean liner, the kind the fills the imaginations of schoolboys," reflected the late ship historian Everett Viez. "She was big, sleek and capped by three of the 'fattest' smokestacks ever to go to sea. Seeing her, she was the absolute definition of a great liner."

Cleverly designed and balanced, the 758-foot-long *Empress*—with her trio of buff-colored, oversized funnels—was created to spend about eight months in trans-ocean service (between Southampton and Quebec City) and then another four months on long, luxurious world cruises from New York.

1188   C. R. Hoffmann, Southampton.   Canadian Pacific Liner. "EMPRESS OF BRITAIN."   42,500 Tons.
CATHAY LOUNGE.

"Shanghai Deco"—the Chinese-inspired Cathay Lounge aboard the *Empress of Britain* of 1931. (*Author's collection*)

STRATHAIRD AND STRATHNAVER (1931)

"They reminded passengers of Britain itself even as they sailed far off, thousands of miles, to places like Bombay, Melbourne and Sydney," recalled P&O captain Philip Jackson. "On the inside, their decor was classically British—lots of woods, soft chairs and sofas, and fireplaces. Every inch of them was absolute British passenger ship." They belonged to P&O and were that company's top ships when completed in 1931.

Above: London all the way to Sydney: period styling aboard P&O's *Strathnaver.* (*Author's collection*)

Left: Two-class cruises on P&O in the 1930s. Voyages were sometimes offered for as little as £1 per day, or $5. (*Author's collection*)

REINA DEL PACIFICO (1931)

"She was the finest ship on the long run between Liverpool, the Caribbean and along the length of the West Coast of South America. She was also one of the best-known ships to use the River Mersey. Everyone, it seemed, had heard of the *Reina Del Pacifico*," said the late ship enthusiast John Havers.

Above: The grand hall and balcony on the *Reina Del Pacifico*. (*Norman Knebel collection*)

Left: Spanish flavor, also on the *Reina Del Pacifico*, which sailed between England, the Caribbean, and the West Coast of South America. (*Author's collection*)

L'ATLANTIQUE (1931)

The 42,512-ton *L'Atlantique* was a true femme fatale—"the beautiful woman doomed to disaster." One of the great Art Deco liners, she burned to death unfortunately just a year after her maiden voyage, on 4 January 1933.

Grand dining! The first-class dining room aboard the *L'Atlantique* of 1931. (*Author's collection*)

LURLINE TRIO (1931-32)

Long lives! "They were great symbols of high-quality American design and construction. They seemed to go on forever. There were three sisters: *Lurline*, *Mariposa*, and *Monterey*. The last of them, the *Monterey*, which last sailed as the Greek *Britanis*, endured for over sixty years. What a great record," said the late maritime historian Frank Braynard.

Pacific sailing on Matson Line's celebrated *Lurline*. (*Norman Knebel collection*)

Sunny retreat: the Lanai "veranda" aboard the *Lurline*. (*Norman Knebel collection*)

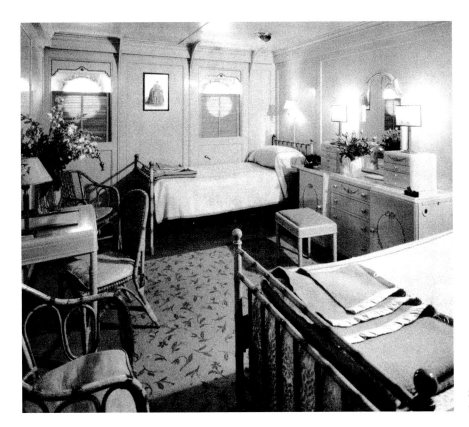

Spacious! A first-class stateroom aboard the *Lurline*. (*Norman Knebel collection*)

A festive departure from Honolulu.
(*Norman Knebel collection*)

CHAMPLAIN (1932)

Although far smaller, this 28,100-tonner was a forerunner to the far larger, quite spectacular *Normandie*. The two ships were completed three years apart—the *Champlain* in 1932 and the *Normandie* in May 1935. A striking ship, she was given fine Art Deco interior styling then well associated to the French Line.

The vast main dining room aboard the French *Champlain*, 1932. (*Norman Knebel collection*)

REX (1932)

It is sadly ironic to note that the glorious *Rex*, flagship of Italy, actually sailed for less than eight years. The onset of World War II shortened the 51,062-grt liner's commercial days and the 880-foot-long ship's lifespan as well. Laid-up in 1940, she was destroyed in an Allied air attack when only twelve years old. Gradually salvaged, her final remains were not removed and scrapped until 1958.

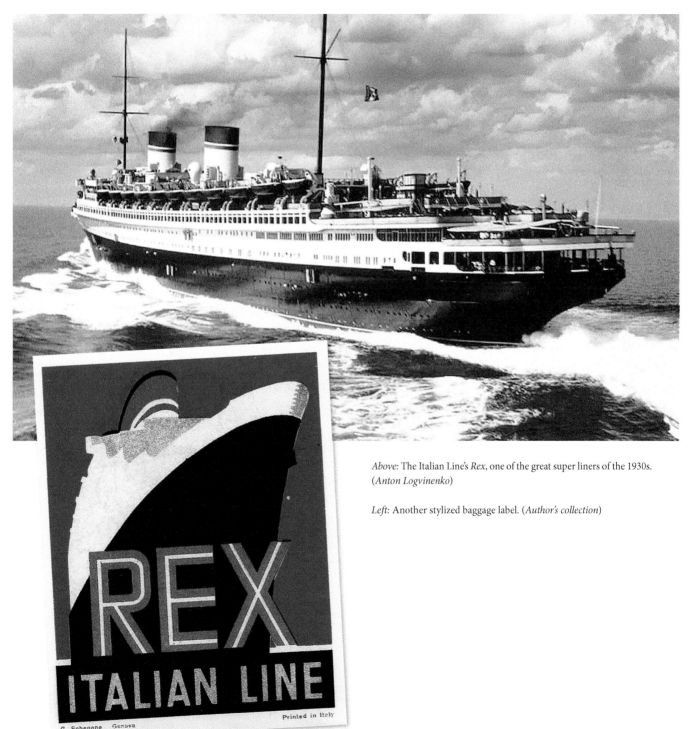

Above: The Italian Line's *Rex*, one of the great super liners of the 1930s. (*Anton Logvinenko*)

Left: Another stylized baggage label. (*Author's collection*)

The Riviera afloat—the first-class pool aboard the *Rex*. (*Photofest*)

CONTE DI SAVOIA (1932)

Similarly, the *Rex*'s running mate on the Naples–Genoa–New York express run, the 48,502-grt *Conte di Savoia*, saw less than eight years of service as well. Also completed in 1932, many thought the *Conte di Savoia* was the better looking, the more striking of the two big Italian liners of the 1930s.

Sadly, the *Conte di Savoia* was burnt out during the war, on 11 September 1943. But her burnt out hull and machinery were thought to have potential for rebuilding in the late 1940s. There was a plan by the Italians to restore and rebuild the ship, but as a 2,500-berth immigrant ship for the Italy–South America run. Both French Line and Holland America Line also thought of buying the remains, but nothing came to pass—those remains of the *Conte di Savoia* were scrapped in 1950.

The long gallery aboard the *Conte di Savoia*. (*Norman Knebel collection*)

SANTA ROSA QUARTET (1932)

Designed by the brilliant William Francis Gibbs, this quartet—created for New York-based Grace Line's Caribbean and South American services—was a prelude to the larger *America* (1940) and then the extraordinary *United States* (1952).

Right: With a roll-back ceiling, dining under tropic skies on the Grace Line's *Santa Rosa* quartet of sisters of 1932–33. (*Author's collection*)

Below: Fun in the Caribbean—cruising became increasingly popular in the 1930s. (*Author's collection*)

WASHINGTON AND MANHATTAN (1932–33)

Completed in 1932–33, they were the largest US-built liners yet. Used on the North Atlantic, this pair sailed between New York, Cobh, Southampton, Le Havre, and Hamburg.

American flavor: the smoking room aboard United States Line's *Washington*. (*Norman Knebel collection*)

QUEEN OF BERMUDA (1933)

She was the most beloved and popular ship ever to make regular sailings to the beautiful island of Bermuda. Popular with the just-married set and her Saturday afternoon sailings, she was soon dubbed "the honeymoon ship."

Two decks in height: the main lounge on the *Queen of Bermuda*. It was $55 for a six-day cruise from New York to Bermuda in 1935. (*Author's collection*)

NORMANDIE (1935)

High luxury! Often she was appraised as the most luxurious liner on the Atlantic—and probably in the world. Commissioned in the spring of 1935, the 82,799-grt *Normandie* was, in many ways, the most sensational, luxurious, and legendary super liner of the twentieth century. Everything about her—from her advanced exterior design to her Art Deco interiors to her superb kitchens—was noteworthy and newsworthy. When she was launched at St Nazaire, there were some 200,000 spectators present. Her godmother was Madame Lebrun, the first lady of France. Numerous names had been suggested for the 1,028-foot-long ship, the new pride of the French fleet, including *General Pershing*, *Napoleon*, and *Jeanne d'Arc*; *La Belle France* was reportedly a strong contender. When *Normandie* was selected, the French Academy insisted that it should be *La Normandie*, but the French Line itself settled on *Normandie*.

Sadly, while celebrated and often copied, the *Normandie* sailed for only for and a half years. An even bigger, possibly more lavish running mate, to be called *Bretagne*, was designed but never built. The 1,972-passenger *Normandie* was abruptly laid-up at New York in August 1939 owing to the possible outbreak of war in Europe. She never sailed again. While being converted to an Allied troopship, carrying some 15,000 soldiers per voyage, she caught fire at her New York pier on 9 February 1942 and later capsized; her salvaged, reduced remains were scrapped in nearby Port Newark, New Jersey, in 1946–47.

Right: Refuge at sea: the exotic Winter Garden on the *Normandie* included caged birds and live greenery. (*Author's collection*)

Below: Magnificence: a stylized rendering of the *Normandie*'s main dining room, which was longer than the Hall of Mirrors at Versailles. (*Author's collection*)

QUEEN MARY (1936)

King George V called her "the stateliest ship in being" at her launching in September 1934. Soon after the traumatic Wall Street Crash in October 1929, even much-loved Atlantic liners such as Cunard's *Aquitania* began to fall on hard times. The Atlantic trade in particular slid steadily into decline: the almost 1 million passengers of, for example, 1930 plummeted to half that number within five years. Cunard, like all ship owners, was worried—very worried. To complicate matters even further, the company had just reviewed the plans of the stately *Aquitania*, then revised and extended them, changed the decorative theme to the new Art Deco style, and ordered a mammoth ship of at least 79,000 tons. She would become the illustrious *Queen Mary*, commissioned in May 1936. The ship went on to become one of the most successful, popular, profitable, and beloved super liners of all time. She lives on, since 1967, as a moored museum and hotel in Long Beach, California.

Above left: The *Queen Mary* was one of the most beloved, illustrious, historic, and heroic liners of all time. (*Author's collection*)

Above right: The main lounge on the *Queen Mary* was pure British Deco, complete with swirl carpets and highly polished woods. (*Author's collection*)

Above: The main lounge also included a stage with orchestra at one end. (*Author's collection*)

Left: Traveling on the *Queen Mary* was described as "being in the best hotel in London except it moved!" (*Cunard*)

Right: Celebrities on board liners were a form of advertising—an endorsement. Here is Errol Flynn on the *Île de France* in 1936. (*Photofest*)

Below: A first-class, twin-bedded outside stateroom with two portholes, sitting area, full bath, and trunk space. For the five-day crossing between New York and Southampton, it was priced at $150. (*Author's collection*)

While many liners struggled during the lean years of the 1930s, the *Queen Mary* was an exception. She averaged 95 percent of capacity. (*Author's collection*)

Queen Mary (1936)

During the dark days of World War II, ships such as the *Queen Mary* were made over as troopships and went from 2,000 passengers per voyage in peace to 15,000 soldiers in wartime. (*Author's collection*)

ORION AND ORCADES (1935–37)

"They brought the style of the great Atlantic liners, that shipboard Art Deco, to the Australian run. They were perhaps the finest liners on the long-haul run between London and Sydney in the 1930s," said Sydney-based ship enthusiast Lindsay Johnstone.

NIEUW AMSTERDAM (1938)

Without any question, she was one of the most beautiful liners ever—both inside and out. When completed in the spring of 1938, this beautiful-looking twin-stacker was immediately proclaimed as one of the best-looking liners afloat. She was the Netherlands' national flagship, built at Rotterdam, and a *tour de force* of mostly modern decorative splendor—incorporating features that had marked the Paris World's Fair of 1937 and were to distinguish the 1939 World's Fair at New York.

Left: Art Deco comes to Australia: it was introduced there by the liner *Orion* in 1937. (*P&O*)

Below: The ceilings of the *Nieuw Amsterdam*'s main restaurant were done in Moroccan leather with Murano chandeliers. (*Author's collection*)

NOORDAM (1938)

Cozy Comfort! The 10,704-ton *Noordam* and her sister, the *Zaandam*, were notable additions to the trans-Atlantic run in the late '30s. The late Captain Cornelius van Herk, who served aboard the *Noordam*, believed that they were "a new concept for their time—all first class, with a mere 125 berths. As combination passenger-cargo liners, they offered a leisurely crossing between Rotterdam and New York of nine days. They appealed particularly to often older, wealthy passengers and who wanted a quiet, longer sea voyage."

Cozy comfort at sea: a side gallery aboard the 148-passenger *Noordam*. (*Author's collection*)

WILHELM GUSTLOFF AND ROBERT LEY (1938–39)

The world's first large, purposeful cruise ships. In the mid-'30s, the Nazi propaganda regime created "Strength Through Joy" cruising—with German passenger liners taking German workers on Nazi-subsidized and organized cruises. It proved successful to their needs such that, by 1937, Hitler's ministers planned no less than ten new liners to be built especially for these cruises. Only two were actually built, however: the 25,484-ton, 1,465-passenger *Wilhelm Gustloff* and then a near-sister, the *Robert Ley*. While both ships were destroyed in the dark days of World War II, the 684-foot-long *Wilhelm Gustloff* officially ranks as the world's first "purposely built large cruise ship."

The social hall aboard the Nazi cruise ship *Wilhelm Gustloff*. (*Author's collection*)

MAURETANIA (1939)

Relief ship to the *Queens*! Introduced in June 1939, this 35,758-ton ship was a smaller version of the *Queen Mary* and a prelude to the giant *Queen Elizabeth*, due in Southampton–New York express service in April 1940. The *Mauretania* could be used as a substitute for the Queens and their five-day crossings, but itself could manage only six-night voyages. She went on, however, to be a very popular ship in her own right—and for off-season, she offered winter cruises as well.

Left: The main lounge aboard the 1939-built *Mauretania*. (*Author's collection*)

Below: A first-class double aboard the *Mauretania*. Note the mounted fan in the upper right. (*Author's collection*)

DOMINION MONARCH (1939)

She was said to be the "most luxurious" ship of her time on the UK–Australia–New Zealand route, carrying only 517 all-first-class passengers in a ship as large as 27,000 tons. Completed in 1939, she was barely in service when called to war duties. She resumed liner sailings until 1962 and did a stint as a hotel ship at Seattle at the end of her time.

All first class to Sydney: the spacious smoking room aboard the *Dominion Monarch*. (*Norman Knebel collection*)

๑5๑

1940-50:
DRINKS IN THE BAR AFTER DINNER

QUEEN ELIZABETH
(1940–46)

The biggest liner afloat! These two Cunard *Queens* were the best known and most successful super liners of all time. However, while always thought of as a pair, even sister ships, they were not identical. The *Queen Mary*, for example, had three funnels; the *Queen Elizabeth* had two. While the 81,237-ton *Queen Mary* was largely a reflection of an earlier standard of ocean liner design, the 83,673-ton *Queen Elizabeth* represented a more contemporary approach. Much of the 2,233-passenger *Elizabeth*'s inspiration came from competing super liners, namely the innovative, exquisite French *Normandie*. The 1,031-foot-long *Queen Elizabeth* remained in Cunard service until 1968, then was sold to become a floating hotel and museum berthed at Fort Lauderdale, Florida. A business failure, the ship was auctioned-off in 1970 to Taiwanese shipping tycoon C. Y. Tung, who planned to transform the world's largest liner into a floating university cruise ship, the *Seawise University*. Unfortunately, in January 1972, on the eve of her maiden voyage, she burned and then capsized in Hong Kong harbor. Her scorched remains could only be cut-up for scrap.

Above: The 850-seat main dining room aboard the *Queen Elizabeth* was done in Canadian Maple. (*Author's collection*)

Opposite page, above: A late Deco styling for the *Queen Elizabeth*'s first-class salon (1946). (*Author's collection*)

MEDIA (1947)

The first post-war Atlantic passenger ship. When the great Cunard Line planned post-World War II replacements, two ships were rather unusual to the illustrious British shipping line: the 250-passenger combination ships *Media* and *Parthia*. They were smaller, slower, and quite intimate. One passenger described life onboard them: "Drinks in the bar before dinner was the highlight of the day's activities!"

Intimate and inviting: the small cocktail lounge on Cunard's 250-passenger *Media*. (*Author's collection*)

DE GRASSE (1947, AFTER REFIT)

This 17,700-ton "intermediate ship," completed in 1924, was sunk in August 1944 but then repaired and restored in 1945–47. She was the first liner to resume French Line service following World War II.

Left: Post-war revival: the return of French Line luxury service with the restored *De Grasse* in 1947. (*Norman Knebel collection*)

Below: The smoking room aboard the refitted *De Grasse*. (*Norman Knebel collection*)

ORCADES (1948)

Rebuilding and renewal: Britain lost many liners in World War II, as did the Orient Line. Post-war rebuilding was all but urgent and included three new liners: the *Orcades* (1948), the *Oronsay* (1951), and the *Orsova* (1954).

HIMALAYA (1949)

Four weeks to Australia: P&O Lines had also lost liners in the war and their replacement program began in 1949 with the 27,955-ton, 1,159-passenger *Himalaya* of 1949. The largest P&O liner to date, the 22-knot ship cut the passage time London and Sydney via Suez from thirty-five to twenty-eight days.

Right: Migrants to Australia: a two-berth room in tourist class on Orient Line's *Orcades,* 1948. (*Author's collection*)

Below: A good book: the first-class library on P&O's *Himalaya* of 1949. (*Author's collection*)

CONTE GRANDE (AFTER 1949 REFIT)

Mentioned previously in Chapter 3, this 1927-built liner was used as the troopship USS *Monticello* during World War II. Returned to the Italian Line in 1947, she was rebuilt and modernized and thereafter used mostly on the Italy–East Coast of South America run.

Left: The return of the largely modernized *Conte Grande* and *Conte Biancamano* to the Italy–South America run in 1949. (*Norman Knebel collection*)

Below: The cabin-class smoking room aboard the refitted *Conte Biancamano*. (*Norman Knebel collection*)

ÎLE DE FRANCE (AFTER 1949)

"More seagulls follow the *Île de France* than any other ship!" After war duties, this glorious French liner was restored—fine décor, superb service, and some of the finest kitchens on all the seas!

The grand lounge of the refitted *Île de France* in 1949. (*Author's collection*)

The library aboard the post-war *Île de France*. (*Author's collection*)

LA MARSEILLAISE (1949)

Colonial style: This 17,300-ton liner was created for French service between Marseilles and colonial Saigon.

French colonial: the first-class Winter Garden aboard the *La Marseillaise*, used on the Marseilles–Saigon colonial service beginning in 1949. (*Author's collection*)

～6～
1950–60:
AIR-CONDITIONING, LIDO DECKS, AND $20-A-DAY TO EUROPE

LIBERTÉ (1950)

Bathing in Champagne! Germany's pre-war *Europa* was thoroughly restyled and refitted as the French *Liberté* in 1947–50. Built in 1930, she had a second life in the '50s as the French flagship and one of the most popular liners on the North Atlantic. But on her first French crossing, in August 1950, her pipes burst and there were water shortages. At New York, reporters questioned the ship's "teething problems." The chief purser was quick to respond: "Yes, there were problems with fresh water but, of course, we are French. We simply bathed in Champagne!"

Revival: following World War II, business for liners resumed and often in great numbers. This view of New York's Luxury Liner Row shows a great collection liners in a view from 1957. *From left to right*: the *Britannic, Queen Elizabeth, Mauretania, Liberté, United States, America, Independence*, and *Vulcania*. (*Port Authority of New York & New Jersey*)

The great main lounge aboard the French flagship *Liberté* as seen after being refitted and remodeled in 1947–50. Previously, the 51,000-ton ship had been the German *Europa*, completed in 1930. (*Author's collection*)

The sumptuous sitting room of a suite aboard the *Liberté*. (*Author's collection*)

RIO TUNUYAN (1951)

"Route of the Rio liners" was advertising for three, very fine, Italian-built combo liners—the *Rio de la Plata*, *Rio Jachal*, and *Rio Tunuyan*—used on the New York–Buenos Aires run for the Argentine State Line.

The bedroom of a suite aboard the 115-passeger *Rio Tunuyan* of the Argentine State Line. (*Author's collection*)

RYNDAM AND MAASDAM (1951–52)

$20 dollars a day to Europe! Holland-America Line looked to the future of trans-Atlantic liner travel when, in 1951–52, they introduced the 15,000-ton sisters *Ryndam* and *Maasdam*. In a new dimension, these 875-passenger ships were divided as 90 percent for tourist class and then only a small, intimate, upper-deck first class for as few as thirty-nine travelers. The comfortable quarters in tourist class had rates that began as low as $20 per person per day.

Tourist-class comfort: the dining room aboard the low-fare *Maasdam*. (*Holland-America Line*)

INDEPENDENCE AND CONSTITUTION (1951)

Air-conditioned throughout! Symbols of post-war American modernity and progress, when the twin sisters *Independence* and *Constitution* were introduced in 1951 for the New York–Mediterranean run, they were the first fully air-conditioned large liners in the world. The ships carried 1,000 passengers, divided in three classes.

Above: Sunny days! The Solarium on the top deck of the *Independence* and *Constitution*. (*Norman Knebel collection*)

Right: American service! Many of the 500 crewmembers of the *Constitution* pose on deck in this 1955 view. (*Author's collection*)

DONGEDYK (1951, AFTER REFIT)

Passenger-cargo liners with limited, more intimate, and often very comfortable quarters were very popular following World War II. Holland-America's *Dongedyk*, originally built in 1929, was thoroughly refitted in 1950–51 for fifty-two all-first-class passengers. Every cabin was outside and had a private shower and toilet. The *Dongedyk* served on the Northern Europe–North American West Coast via Panama run.

A double-bedded cabin aboard the combo ship *Dongedyk*. (*Holland-America Line*)

GIULIO CESARE AND AUGUSTUS (1951–52)

Italian resurgence: Italy lost all but four of its big pre-war liners and so, in the late '40s, began to plan for replacements. The first of these were the 27,000-ton, 1,180-passenger pair *Giulio Cesare* and *Augustus*. They were created purposely for the then-booming three-class liner trade between Naples, Genoa, Cannes, Barcelona, and Lisbon over to Rio de Janeiro, Santos, Montevideo, and Buenos Aires.

New liners! The Italian twins *Giulio Cesare* and *Augustus* of 1951–52 were the sensations of their day on the busy Italy–South America run. (*Norman Knebel collection*)

Above: After dinner: dancing in the cabin-class ballroom aboard the *Giulio Cesare*. (*Author's collection*)

Left: Sleek, Italian post-war décor aboard the *Giulio Cesare*. (*Author's collection*)

Below: Highly polished linoleum: the first-class entrance foyer on the *Giulio Cesare*. (*Author's collection*)

UNITED STATES (1952)

The U.S. Government had been deeply impressed by the use, during World War II, of such liners as the *Queen Mary* and *Queen Elizabeth* being adapted to carry 15,000 military personnel. So, in the late '40s, and fearful that another major conflict might erupt, the Americans decided to build a very advanced trans-Atlantic super liner that, above all, could easily be converted into an emergency troopship. It emerged in June 1952 as the 53,329-ton, $75 million *United States*. She was exceptionally safe, very modern, and tremendously powerful. She took the Blue Riband from the *Queen Mary* with an average speed of 36 knots, reached 39 knots at times, and, during sea trials, managed a remarkable 43 knots for a short time. During the '50s, the *United States* was one of the most popular liners on the North Atlantic. Laid-up in 1969, she has been idle ever since.

Above: American mid-century décor: the ballroom aboard the extraordinary *United States*. (*Author's collection*)

Right: The fastest way to Europe on the speedy *United States*. (*Norman Knebel collection*)

ANDREA DORIA AND CRISTOFORO COLOMBO (1952–54)

Italian renaissance! The 29,000-ton sister ships *Andrea Doria* and *Cristoforo Colombo* were the first new national liners built by the Italian Line for the New York trade after World War II. They were to symbolize—primarily to the Americans—that the Italian merchant marine was reborn. Although smaller in size than the Italian ships of state in the '30s, these new, 1,241-berth liners featured some of the best in post-war Italian art and decoration. The 700-foot-long *Andrea Doria* is, however, best remembered for her tragic end. She sank off Nantucket in July 1956, after colliding with the Swedish liner *Stockholm*.

Sunny days to the Mediterranean: the pool decks, one for each class, on the *Cristoforo Colombo*. (*Holiday Magazine*)

Horse-racing after dinner onboard the *Andrea Doria*. (*Norman Knebel collection*)

Fun in the sun! The tourist-class lido deck on the *Andrea Doria*. (*Norman Knebel collection*)

CAMBODGE TRIO (1953–54)

On the run to Saigon: this 13,500-ton ship and her two sisters, *Laos* and *Viet-Nam*, ran monthly sailings from Marseilles to the Far East via Suez. Operated by Messageries Maritimes, they carried some 450 passengers in three classes.

The first-class main lounge on the French *Cambodge*, sailing from Marseilles to the likes of Saigon, Singapore, and Hong Kong. (*Author's collection*)

The cocktail lounge aboard Hamburg-America Line's combo ship *Hamburg*. (*Author's collection*)

HAMBURG CLASS (1954)

German businessmen: this ship and her five sisters (the *Frankfurt*, *Hannover*, *Bayernstein*, *Hessenstein*, and *Schwabenstein*) were very fine passenger-cargo liners that carried eighty-six all-first-class travelers on the long-haul run from Northern Europe out to the Far East. They were especially popular with businessmen.

SAXONIA CLASS (1954–57)

Cunard to Canada! Cunard's final pure trans-Atlantic liners were in fact a quartet of 23,000-tonners—the *Saxonia*, *Ivernia*, *Carinthia*, and *Sylvania*—created purposely for the run to Eastern Canada—to Quebec City and Montreal.

Sailing to Canada: the tourist-class main lounge on the 1954-built *Saxonia* of Cunard. (*Author's collection*)

Trans-Atlantic travel especially boomed by the mid-1950s. There were hundreds of crossings each year, highlighted by the five-night crossings between Southampton, Cherbourg, and New York on the mighty *Queen Elizabeth* and *Queen Mary*. (*Author's collection*)

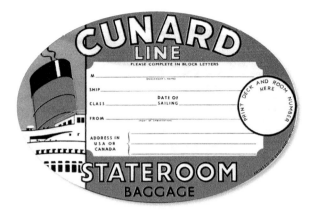

Luggage bound for New York! (*Author's collection*)

Above: Elegance on Cunard and its liners. (*Author's collection*)

Right: Festive occasion: sailing day from New York's Pier 90 aboard the *Mauretania*. (*Author's collection*)

Summer weather allowed for deck games aboard Atlantic liners. (*Author's collection*)

Winter crossings could be stormy and turbulent. (*Author's collection*)

Afternoon tea along the enclosed Promenade Deck. (*Author's collection*)

There were celebrities aboard almost every crossing of the big and famous Atlantic liners—such as Elizabeth Taylor on the *Queen Elizabeth*. (*Cunard*)

Rita Hayworth strikes-up a bon voyage pose. (*Cunard*)

The duke and duchess of Windsor crossed four times a year on the *United States*. (*Photofest*)

Grace Kelly sailed to her royal wedding to Prince Rainier, from New York to Monte Carlo, on the *Independence* in April 1956. (*Photofest*)

UIGE (1954)

Portugese colonial service: this Belgian-built, 10,000-tonner was one of the last ships created for colonial service. Carrying seventy-eight in first class and nearly 500 in third class, she traded between Lisbon and Portugese West Africa.

Basic and austere: third-class quarters on the Portuguese colonial passenger ship *Uige*. (*Companhia Colonial*)

STATENDAM (1957)

The tourist-class dominance of accommodations on Holland-America's *Ryndam* and *Maasdam* was such a great success in the early '50s that the company considered an even larger, improved version of these ships. Designs were begun in 1954. It was decided that the new ship would be named *Statendam* and that 90 percent of her tourist class cabins were fitted with private showers and toilets.

A first-class twin-bedded cabin on the *Statendam* of 1957. (*Holland-America Line*)

FEDERICO "C" (1958)

Highly successful from its first passenger sailings in 1948, Italy's Costa Line created their first new build in the form of the 20,400-ton, 1,279-passenger *Federico "C"* of 1958. Following in the wake of the likes of the earlier *Andrea Doria*, the Genoa shipbuilders again produced a very modern ship.

Sleek Italian styling: the first-class ballroom on the Costa Line's *Federico "C"*. (*Author's collection*)

Italian liners such as the *Federico "C"* were noted for their umbrella-lined lido decks. (*Author's collection*)

HANSEATIC (AFTER 1958 REFIT)

Rebuilding older liners became very popular in the '50s and '60s. One of the best conversions was remaking Britain's three-funnel *Empress of Scotland* over, in 1958, as the twin-funnel *Hanseatic* for West Germany's Hamburg-Atlantic Line.

The long gallery/hall on the refitted *Hanseatic*, the former *Empress of Scotland*. (*Author's collection*)

ROTTERDAM (1959)

Dutch ship of state: when Holland-America's *Rotterdam* was commissioned in the summer of 1959, she was another superb ship of state—the flagship for both her country and her owners. On her twelve passenger decks, there were over fifteen public rooms (making extensive use of woods such as Bangkok teak, Japanese ash wood, and French walnut), indoor as well as outdoor swimming pools, and the largest theater afloat, seating 607. The 38,645-ton *Rotterdam* has been preserved and is berthed in Rotterdam harbor for use as a hotel, museum, convention, and entertainment center.

One of the two main dining rooms aboard the 1959-built, Dutch flagship *Rotterdam*. (*Holland-America Line*)

Above: Midnight buffets were once rituals on ocean liners. (*Holland-America Line*)

Left: Elegance: the *Rotterdam*'s first-class ballroom. (*Author's collection*)

British contemporary: the first-class smoking room on the *Amazon* of 1959. (*Author's collection*)

AMAZON (1959)

The last British passenger ships built to carry passengers in three classes, the 20,300-ton *Amazon* and her sisters—the *Aragon* and the *Arlanza*—were designed purposely to carry passengers (almost 500 in all) as well as cargo on the UK–East Coast of South America run.

~7~
1960-70:
LAST OF A KIND

CANBERRA (1961)

P&O's 45,733-ton, 2,272-bed *Canberra*—commissioned in the spring of 1961—is the largest liner ever built for a service other than the Atlantic. As the flagship of the P&O fleet (which had the world's largest passenger fleet in 1960), she carried more passengers than the other company's liners and had to be very fast and offer innovative, modern, yet comfortable accommodations. Considering her future blend of Australian, trans-Pacific, and long world voyages, it was thought that she would cater primarily to British and American passengers. The Britons liked modernity without extremes; the Americans preferred modernity almost to excess. A suitable balance had to be established.

Sixties simplicity: A first-class suite aboard P&O's *Canberra*, 1961. (*P&O*)

INFANTE DOM HENRIQUE (1961)

The 23,306-ton *Infante Dom Henrique* of Portugal's Colonial Navigation Co. was the last of the colonial liners. Belgian-built, she was designed primarily to sail between Lisbon and the Portuguese-African outposts of Angola and Mozambique. However, in all other ways, she was a radical change from earlier steamers that plied such trades. Gone were the dark-paneled lounges and verandas, the overhead fans, and the potted palms. Gone also were three or four classes of passengers. Instead, there was a small, top-deck first class and then a large, more comfortable tourist class.

The first-class main lounge aboard the Portuguese *Infante Dom Henrique*. (*Companhia Colonial*)

FRANCE (1962)

The French Line's *France* was the last superliner designed to spend most of her year in regular North Atlantic service. However, by the time of her maiden crossing, in February 1962, the jet had already posed unbeatable competition. At best, the 66,348-ton, 1,944-passenger *France* would cater to those who still yearned for a more leisurely, more luxurious way to cross the ocean. In quick time, the $80 million ship developed an impeccable reputation based on a blend of legendary French Line service and superb cooking.

Bound for Le Havre: a baggage label for the legendary *France* of 1962. (*Author's collection*)

A stairwell and landing aboard the *France*. (*French Line*)

Stylized French Line advertising. (*Author's collection*)

The bedroom of a first-class suite on the *France* and priced from $2,000 per person for the five-day crossings in 1965. (*Author's collection*)

SAVANNAH (1964)

To display and promote the use of nuclear power for peaceful purposes, the U.S. Government produced the sixty-passenger combo liner *Savannah*. Her first voyage was from New York to Bremerhaven in June 1964.

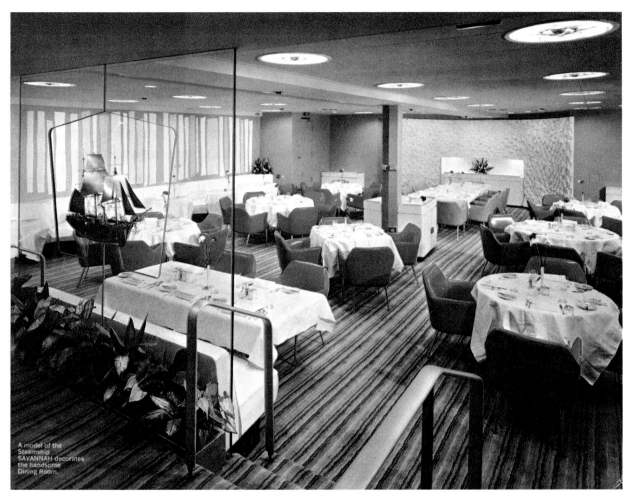

The dining room aboard the nuclear-powered *Savannah*. (*Author's collection*)

MICHELANGELO AND RAFFAELLO (1965)

Despite the huge and devastating inroads of the airlines on trans-Atlantic travel, the Italian Line built not one but two super liners, the 45,900-ton *Michelangelo* and *Raffaello* super liners as late as 1965. Carrying up to 1,775 passengers each, they were designed for the Naples–Genoa–New York express run and part-time winter cruising. The $120 million pair survived, however, for only ten years.

Left: Italian Line to the Mediterranean and on cruises. (*Author's collection*)

Below: A first-class suite on the *Michelangelo*. (*Author's collection*)

OCEANIC (1965)

By the mid-'60s, cruising was the future for passenger liners. While being built in Italy and intended for Hamburg–Montreal service in summers, the role of Home Lines' extravagant new flagship *Oceanic* was rethought. Instead, she would cruise all year long—on seven-day voyages between New York and Nassau.

Left: The huge, but retractable Magrodome covering two pools and the vast lido deck on the innovative *Oceanic* of 1965. (*Author's collection*)

Below: An aerial view of the Magrodome aboard the *Oceanic*. (*Moran Towing & Transportation Co.*)

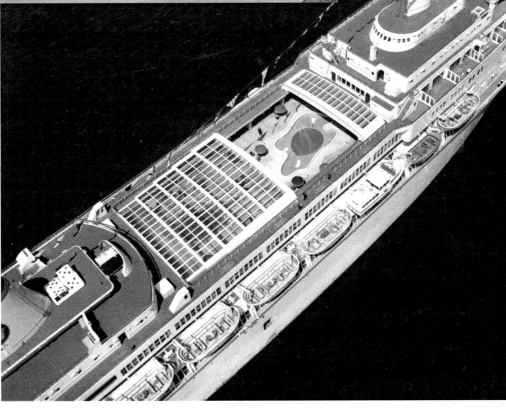

EUGENIO "C" (1966)

On the South Atlantic run between Italy and South America, Italy's Costa Line persisted with tradition. When the 30,567-grt *Eugenio "C"* entered service in 1966, she carried up to 1,636 passengers in three classes: first, cabin, and tourist.

The sweeping first-class ballroom on Costa's *Eugenio "C"* of 1966. (*Author's collection*)

QUEEN ELIZABETH 2 (1969)

When Cunard first decided to replace the aging *Queen Mary* and *Queen Elizabeth* in the early '60s, it thought of a conventional, three-class design. Then, based on considerations of airline competition and the growth of tropical cruising, the concept of the new liner was worked. The 65,863-ton ship emerged as the *Queen Elizabeth 2*, christened by Queen Elizabeth II in September 1967 and commissioned in May 1969. Carrying up to 2,005 passengers, the *QE2* was a remarkable success: she steamed more miles, carried more passengers, visited more ports, and served longer than any other big liner. Retired by Cunard after thirty-nine years of service in November 2008, she was sold to buyers in Dubai and, after a long wait, finally opened as a moored hotel in April 2018.

Left: Legendary liners: the *Queen Mary 2* (left) and the *Queen Elizabeth* departing from New York in October 2008. (*Cunard*)

Below: The main ballroom aboard the *Queen Elizabeth 2*. (*Author's collection*)

The *QE2*'s entrance foyer/lobby was quite futuristic looking for the late '60s. (*Author's collection*)

8

1970 AND BEYOND:
FLOATING HOTELS—THE MOVING RESORTS

SONG OF NORWAY (1970)

At the beginning of the new North American cruise boom, this 876-berth ship for the first ship for then newly created Royal Caribbean Lines in 1970. One of three sister ships and used in seven-day Caribbean cruising from Miami, they were among the "pioneer ships" of today's cruise industry.

Ships such as the 1970-built *Song of Norway* ushered in a new generation of newly built, mass-market cruise ships. One critic described their décor as "Low ceilings, metallic, almost airport-like." (*Royal Caribbean Cruise Lines*)

Cabins became smaller, more compact and encouraged passengers to spend more time on deck, in activities, spending more money. (*Royal Caribbean Cruise Lines*)

NIEUW AMSTERDAM AND NOORDAM (1983–84)

These fine, French-built liners, commissioned in 1983–84, were created for year-round cruising in North America. Their décor was especially noteworthy: it incorporated vintage antiques in a contemporary modern setting.

Above: In 1983–84, Holland-America Line was among the first to return to shipboard elegance by blending contemporary décor with historical fittings such as the age of early discovery and navigation on their *Nieuw Amsterdam*. (*Holland-America Line*)

SOVEREIGN OF THE SEAS (1988)

Royal Caribbean Cruise Lines progressed with the vast expansion of cruising with three new sisterships by 1987. The 73,129-ton, 2,673-passenger *Sovereign of the Seas*—used in Miami–Caribbean cruising—then ranked as the largest liner yet built for cruising.

Right: The concept of the impressive, multi-deck lobby took a big step with the *Sovereign of the Seas* in 1987. Gleaming in glass and brass, it reached six decks in height. (*Royal Caribbean Cruise Lines*)

FANTASY (1990)

Beginning in 1972, Miami-based Carnival Cruise Lines had had phenomenal success and growth. Within thirty years, the company had 43,000 staff and was carrying 4½ million passengers a year. One highpoint was the addition of no less than eight 70,000-ton, 2,600-passenger ships between 1990 and 1998: the *Fantasy*, *Ecstasy*, *Fascination*, *Imagination*, *Inspiration*, *Paradise*, *Sensation*, and *Elation*.

Right: Carnival Cruise Lines opted for a "fun at sea" concept and design with lots of color, bright neon and eye-catching, thematic, Las Vegas-style décor. (*Carnival Cruise Lines*)

Below: After-dinner shows have reached Broadway and West End levels. Overall, the current cruise passenger must be "wowed" by the ship itself and what it has to offer. (*Carnival Cruise Lines*)

Vast sun, pool, and lido decks are extremely popular on current cruise ships such as this panoramic view on Carnival's Fascination. (*Carnival Cruise Lines*)

ROTTERDAM (1998)

After Holland-America Line ended its trans-Atlantic services in 1971, the company turned completely to cruising. A new fleet of ships was added and, by 1998, the 61,800-ton, 1,400-bed *Rotterdam* was their largest and the company flagship. Highly successful, by 2018, the company operated fifteen cruise ships.

Glitter & sparkle: the lobby of Holland-America's *Rotterdam*. The first impression is considered, by current cruise lines and their designers, to be very important. (*Carnival Cruise Lines*)

VOYAGER OF THE SEAS (1999)

As the cruise continued to expand, Royal Caribbean's 137,200-ton, 3,840-passenger *Voyager of the Seas*—completed in 1999—ranked as the largest passenger liner yet built. One of five sister ships, she has, however, been surpassed, in 2017, by the likes of the same company's 228,000-ton, 6,800-berth *Symphony of the Seas*.

The three-deck level dining room aboard the *Voyager of the Seas* class. (*Royal Caribbean Cruise Lines*)

QUEEN MARY 2 (2004)

Highlighted as the largest trans-Atlantic liner ever built, the 2,600-passenger *Queen Mary 2* divides her year between Southampton–New York crossings and cruises. In light of her other distinctions and illustrious Cunard history, she is the most famous liner afloat in 2020.

Above: Classical style: restful and relaxing, the chart room on the *Queen Mary 2*. (*Author's collection*)

Right: The main lobby and entrance foyer on the *Queen Mary 2*. (*Author's ollection*)

QUEEN VICTORIA (2006)

The first 90,000-tonner intended for Cunard. The *Queen Victoria* never materialized, and was instead diverted to P&O Cruises and completed as their *Arcadia*. This 2,100-passenger ship was completed later, in 2007, and has been used primarily for the British cruise market, which had become the second largest after North America by 2010.

The popular ballroom on Cunard's *Queen Victoria*. (*Author's collection*)

The lobby of the current *Queen Elizabeth* with a wall design depicting the original *Queen Elizabeth*. (*Author's collection*)

QUEEN ELIZABETH (2010)

This slightly different version of the *Queen Victoria* follows in the naming tradition of the original *Queen Elizabeth* (1940) and then the *Queen Elizabeth 2* (1969). A 92,000-tonner, she was named by Her Majesty Queen Elizabeth II.

ALLURE OF THE SEAS (2010)

By 2020, Royal Caribbean remained the second largest cruise operator and continued to expand (with no less than eight more, and often increasingly bigger, cruise liners on order). In 2009–10, the company added two new ships that were again the biggest afloat—the 225,000-ton, 6,300-passenger sisters *Oasis of the Seas* and *Allure of the Seas*.

Novelty and attraction: a bar that rises and lowers three decks aboard the *Allure of the Seas*. (*Author's collection*)

MSC DIVINA (2012)

After first entering the cruise business in 1984, Italian-owned MSC Cruises is today (2020) the biggest cruise operator in all Europe. Owning some fifteen cruise ships (as well as over 400 cargo ships), the company has been highly progressive—building one new cruise ship per year. The 139,000-ton *MSC Divina*, originally to have been called *MSC Favolosa*, was added in 2012 and can carry almost 4,000 passengers.

It is said to be the largest showroom afloat, aboard MSC Cruises' *MSC Divina*. (*Author's collection*)

A double cabin on the *MSC Divina*. (*MSC Cruises*)

CARNIVAL HORIZON (2018)

By 2020, cruising was booming. Alone, over 125 new ships were either being built or on the design tables, and more travelers are taking to the high seas than ever. Further growth in passengers is projected:

2007: 15.6 million   **2017:** 25.8 million   **2018:** 26.5 million   **2027:** estimated 40 million

Miami-headquartered Carnival Corporation is by far the leader in the industry—owning some twelve different cruise ships and altogether well over 100 ships. These liners ply just about every cruise run; alone, Carnival controls 49.5 percent of the entire worldwide cruise market.

In 2018, one of its subsidiaries, Carnival Cruise Lines, commissioned its largest ship yet: the 133,000-ton, 3,950-passenger *Carnival Horizon*. Decoratively innovative in places, this $850 million ship is just a hint of many interesting passenger ships, those modern-day "floating hotels," to come.

Above: The Havana Club aboard the *Carnival Horizon* (2018). (*Author's collection*)

Right: As more and more cruise ships enter service, existing ones must be made more competitive, upgraded, and modernized. Here, in 2017, the giant *Queen Mary 2* is extensively refitted at a Hamburg shipyard. Cunard dubbed it "re-mastering." Indeed, the long history of liners and their interiors will continue.

BIBLIOGRAPHY

Kludas, A., *Great Passenger Ships of the World* (Vols. 1–5); *Great Passenger Ships of the World* (Wellingborough, Northamptonshire: Patrick Stephens Ltd, 1984, 1992); *Great Passenger Ships of the World* (Hamburg: Koehlers Publishing Co., 1987, 1997)

Kludas, A., Heine, F., and Lose, F., *The Great Passenger Ships of the World* (Hamburg: Koehlers Publishing Co., 2002, 2006)

Miller, W. H., *The Fabulous Interiors of the Great Ocean Liners* (New York: Dover Publications Inc., 1985); *Pictorial Encyclopedia of Ocean Liners 1860–1994* (New York: Dover Publications, 1995)

Official Steamship Guide (New York City: Transportation Guides Inc., 1953–63)